SO-ARN-057

BBC Children's Books
Published by the Penguin Group
Penguin Books Ltd, 80 Strand, London, WC2R 0RL, England
Penguin Group (Australia) Ltd, 250 Camberwell Road, Camberwell, Victoria 3124, Australia (a division of Pearson Australia Group Pty Ltd)
Canada, India, New Zealand, South Africa

Published by BBC Children's Books, 2013
Text and design © Children's Character Books, 2013

001 – 10 9 8 7 6 5 4 3 2 1

Written by Dan Newman and Sam Philip
Pole to Pole Challenge written by Kevin Pettman and illustrated by Kevin Hopgood
With thanks to Thomas Evans

ISBN: 9781405912778

Printed in Italy

Additional picture credits: Shutterstock.com

TopGear Annual 2014

Contents

Introduction

Hello everyone – welcome back! It's been a busy year for middle-aged men who like to muck about with cars. What were the highs and lows for Jeremy, Richard, James and the Stig?

AAARGH! Help, help, HELP!!

This isn't just an engine, it's a **force of nature!**

YES! Sorry mate, **that was close.**

It's just an **amazing combination** of **nimbleness** and **brute force!**

I hate being a Mini, I have to sleep outside [and a **dog weed** on **my wheel** last night], and all the **big cars steal** my petrol money.

It's called the **Onyx**, it **looks** absolutely **fantastic,** and you will notice that some of the **bodywork is** made of **copper.** Just like the **boiler tubes** on a **Gresley A4 Streamliner Pacific locomotive.**

This is weird now. If I take this off and I'm parked, **I shall be amazed.**

That is a **savage, savage thing.** I **can't get enough** of that. **I'm going to do it again!**

An **intelligent machine driven** by a **computer** has been **beaten** by an **intelligent machine driven** by a **human being,** which is **as it should be.**

Everything about the **GT86** is **immediate** and **brilliant. And I haven't got** to the **best bit yet!**

This car, finally, **feels like a Bentley** should. It's not the magnitude of the power, it's the way it's turned into speed. You get a **discreet 'ahem' from** the butler, and then this **big aristocratic whoomp in the kidneys.**

You idiot! It's ruined! I wet myself AGAIN!

Loserr! Ha haa! You look a bit **tired, mate.**

If somebody were to offer me the **choice of any car** that had **ever been made,** ever, I **would take a** dark blue **LFA.** I'm gonna say it: **it's the best car I've ever driven.** It really is.

I'm going to put my **hand on** my **heart,** and say that this is the **best** Top Gear **adventure we've ever had.**

JEREMY'S FAVOURITE CARS

The Top Gear presenters have strong opinions about many things, but cars are their true love. So which ones do the boys really really rate?

Mercedes CLK Black Series

'This is the car for when it's four in the morning and you've the entire British road network to yourself,' grinned Clarkson when he tested the bonkers CLK Black back in 2008. Costing a cool £100,000 and even harder, faster and noisier than the other daft creations of Merc's AMG department, the Black impressed Clarkson so much that he bought one!

Lamborghini Aventador

Why does Clarkson love the Aventador? No, not because it's packing a 691bhp V12, or because it's fast enough to travel through time. Not even because it's so low and pointy that it looks like it might slice you in half just for looking at it. But because it spits blue flames out of its exhaust, and is therefore the greatest car in the world.

VRMM VRMM VRMM

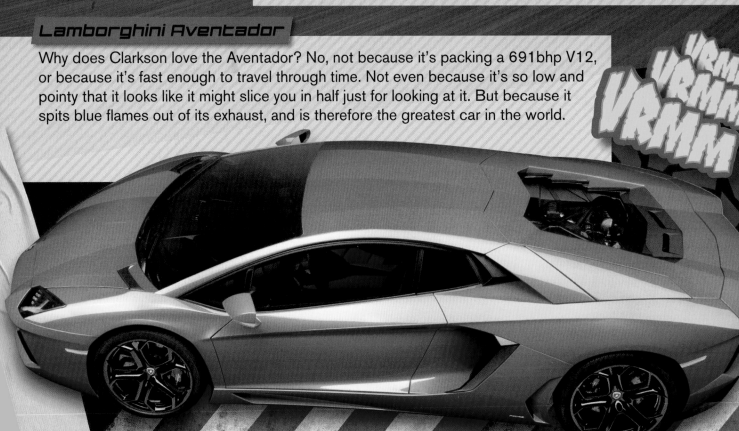

Jaguar E-Type

Clarkson reckons the sleek Jaguar – first seen in 1961 – is the most beautiful car ever created, and it's hard to argue with his opinion. Driving one in 2011 to celebrate the E-Type's fiftieth anniversary, he called it 'beguiling, bewitching and beautiful… almost certainly the last truly great thing that Britain made.' Trouble is, buying one in mint condition will set you back hundreds of thousands…

Ariel Atom

If you'd spent the last couple of decades sharing a studio with Hammond and May, you'd probably have a few wrinkles too. But Jeremy discovered a far simpler way of getting a facelift than expensive surgery or smelly moisturisers: a blast down the runway in the face-bending Ariel Atom…

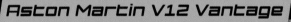

Aston Martin V12 Vantage

There's not much that reduces loudmouth Clarkson to silence. But the stunning V12 Vantage – created by stuffing Aston's biggest engine into its smallest car – had even JC lost for words when he tested it in series 13. 'It's an Aston Martin Vantage with a V12 engine,' was all he could manage. 'What do you think it's going to be like?' Pretty amazing, was the answer. Though he worried the V12 Vantage might be the end of an era, for once Clarkson was wrong: there have been plenty more big-engined, beautiful Astons since…

Ford GT

Clarkson has always loved the original Ford GT40, a supercar introduced in 1964 which won the Le Mans 24 Hours race four times. Unfortunately, because the GT40 stood just forty inches tall, it was too small for him to ever squeeze into. Happily, in 2005, Ford introduced a new GT, which looked just like the original but was precisely three inches taller, making it large enough for Jeremy to squeeze inside. Clarkson was so taken by the new GT40's mix of brutal V8 power and 1960s cool that he decided to buy one. OK, it didn't prove very reliable, but at least it looked good…

JAMES' FAVOURITE CARS

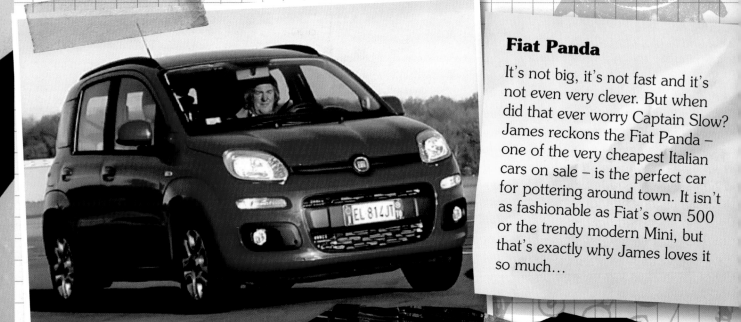

Fiat Panda

It's not big, it's not fast and it's not even very clever. But when did that ever worry Captain Slow? James reckons the Fiat Panda – one of the very cheapest Italian cars on sale – is the perfect car for pottering around town. It isn't as fashionable as Fiat's own 500 or the trendy modern Mini, but that's exactly why James loves it so much…

Bugatti Veyron Super Sport

How do you shift a nickname like 'Captain Slow'? By doing 259mph in the fastest production car in history, that's how. When James set a new world record in the 1200bhp Veyron SS – the even-more-powerful, even-faster version of Bugatti's world-beating hypercar – he proved he could do much more than pootle slowly around. Of course, that hasn't stopped Richard and Jeremy from still calling him Captain Slow…

CAPTAIN SLOW

Ferrari 250 California

'This is the realisation of a childhood dream,' whooped James when he convinced millionaire DJ Chris Evans to lend him his Ferrari 250. 'It's fantastic!' The 250 California first hit the roads in 1957, but it wasn't until 2012 that James finally got to drive his dream car. And it was every bit as good as he hoped: pity buying one would set him back £5.6 million!

Rolls-Royce Corniche

Giant, stately and really-not-very-fast, the Corniche – which debuted way back in 1971 – is a limousine for the discerning gentleman. No surprise, then, that it's a favourite not only of piano-bashing crooner Elton John, but also the stately, not-very-fast James May. In fact, the Corniche is such a favourite of James May that he actually bought one a few years ago to do battle with Clarkson's Mercedes Grosser…

Dacia Sandero

Good news! James's favourite budget Romanian runabout is finally on sale in the UK, and it's as cheap as he could ever have hoped. A brand new Sandero costs less than £6,000, officially making it the lowest-priced car on sale in the UK and the perfect city runabout for penny-pinching May. In fact, he's already calculated that he could buy nearly a thousand Sanderos for the price of one Ferrari 250 California!

RICHARD'S FAVOURITE CARS

Ford Mustang

Because Hammond is a secret American (according to Jeremy), he loves the original US muscle car, the tyre-smokin' Ford Mustang. Not the modern one, though – with technology including 'electronics' and 'working brakes' – that one's far too safe for our fearless Hamster. Instead, Hammond's perfect Mustang is the immaculate 1960s original he tested on the show in 2007… a car that belonged to him!

VRRRAAAAAAHHH
VRRRAAAAAAHHH

Marauder

Most normal people's ideal city car would be something small, cheap and wieldy: a Toyota iQ, maybe, or a Mini. But Hammond isn't a normal person. His perfect city car weighs ten tonnes, measures twenty-one feet from nose to tail and allows you to drive straight through brick walls without noticing. Plenty of space in the back for your shopping, too…

Ferrari F40 and Porsche 959

These were the two greatest supercars of the 1980s. When the Porsche 959 arrived in 1986, it was the fastest car the world had ever seen, capable of 197mph and boasting technology never before seen. But just a year later, the amazing Ferrari F40 appeared to steal the 959's crown, with a 201mph top speed and a lethal 478bhp twin-turbo V8. Richard finally managed to get both together on the *TG* test track in 2011, and he wasn't disappointed. 'So often you shouldn't drive your heroes,' he grinned, 'but this is better than I could have imagined!' Richard couldn't pick between these two amazing supercars, so they're both in his dream garage...

Land Rover Defender

The Defender is built in the Midlands and loved by welly-wearing countryfolk around the world. Hammond grew up in the Midlands and now lives in the depths of the countryside, so it's no surprise he loves the dependable old Defender. In fact, he loves the Defender so much that he's got half a dozen rusty, leaky 'second-hand' versions sitting in his garage, ready for repair. Good news: the simple Defender is easy to fix with nothing more than a few spanners and a big hammer!

Oliver

There are only two rules in the world of *Top Gear*: never go on a caravanning holiday, and never name your car. But on the boys' big adventure across Botswana, Hammond fell so in love with his rusty Opel Kadett that he christened it Oliver. Shameful behaviour from a TG presenter, and, even worse, Hammond then had Oliver shipped home so they could spend some quality time together on British shores. What a softie!

I ♥ OLIVER

THE STIG'S FAVOURITE CARS

Ariel Atom V8

This bonkers 500bhp lightweight helped The Stig set one of the fastest laps the *Top Gear* test track has ever seen, and it's just the sort of car our white-suited mystery man adores: blisteringly quick, no electronic aids and not to be tackled by anyone with less than superhuman skills.

Koenigsegg CCX (with *Top Gear* wing)

When he tested it in original form, the CCX was too wild even for our super-skilled tame racing driver, firing him into a tyre barrier. But with a special *Top Gear*-designed wing fitted to keep the rear tyres to the track, The Stig wrestled the CCX to a smokingly fast lap. Some say he has erased all evidence of the original CCX crash from the BBC archives…

Caterham R500

The R500 is one of the fastest Caterhams ever, and about as comfortable as being trapped in a washing machine on spin cycle with a few hundred ice cubes; cold, dizzying, painful and likely to end in a trip to hospital. Which is exactly why The Stig – a being who feels no pain – loves the safety-free R500 very much. Get it wrong, and this lightweight Brit will spit you straight off the track… but Stiggy doesn't know the meaning of 'getting it wrong'.

A Duck

OK, so the small water-loving bird isn't (technically) a car, but The Stig loves ducks so very much that he'd be deeply angry if they weren't included in his dream garage. No one knows whether he eats them, keeps them as pets or has long conversations with them about French literature. All we know is, there's always a small gaggle of them waiting outside his 'dressing room' at the *Top Gear* studio…

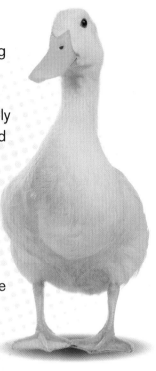

Chevrolet Corvette

If a normal human thrashed the Audi R8 and Chevrolet Corvette back-to-back around the *Top Gear* test track, he or she would go much faster in the four-wheel drive, friendly Audi. But The Stig, because he doesn't care for friendly cars, went faster in the snappy, slidey, rear-wheel drive Corvette. Sure, the Audi has a better sat nav, but so far as we can tell, the Stig seems to have an inbuilt, foolproof navigation system of his own…

Noble M600

No one knows for sure if The Stig is British, or even hails from this planet. But he seems to have a fondness for Brit-built cars, especially if they're as adrenaline-pumping as the hyperspeed Noble. Built in a shed in Leicestershire, and packing a 650bhp twin-turbo V8 and an interior with all the luxury of a small prison cell, this is a car as His Stigness likes 'em: no frills and all thrills. Stand back and watch the tyres sizzle…

Porsche GT2 RS

There are two things that make a supercar perfect for the fearless Lord Stig: lots of power, and rear-wheel drive. And Porsche's fearsome GT2 – the most potent 911 in the model's fifty-year history – is pretty much as rear-wheel drive and powerful as they come, with a turbocharged 620bhp engine lurking behind the driver. They call it the 'Widowmaker', but nicknames like that don't scare The Stig!

The *TopGear* CAROMATIC SELECTIONATOR

Choosing cars is so difficult – there are just so many of them. Luckily, *Top Gear* is here to help. Just answer the questions and end up with the perfect vehicle for you.

START

How do you feel about roads?

Love them. They're the only things I ever drive on.

How much money have you got?

Enough to buy a football every day.

Enough to buy a footballer every day.

They're all right I suppose, if there's nothing better.

Are you handy with your, er, hands? Can you fix stuff?

I have a full set of spanners that I keep in labelled drawers and I know how to use them.

If hitting something with a hammer doesn't work, I buy a new one.

I could if I had to, on a nice day, but I'd rather be in the garage.

And are you certain you don't want to use roads?

What do you take with you on a trip?

Just me, the shopping, the dogs, a surfboard, tent, sleeping bags...

Just me.

Just me and the shopping.

You want a **4x4**, like a Range Rover. Take it anywhere, carry anything.

You should get an **old classic** – something you can tinker with and polish, and (very occasionally) take for a gentle drive. How about an old Rolls-Royce?

You want a **trackday car** – tiny, powerful and useless in the rain, like the Caterham 7 Superlight R500.

You need a **hot hatch** – something like a Citroen DS3 Racing. Useful *and* fun, especially if you ever get to drive the Monaco Grand Prix circuit.

16

Do you mind bad weather?

Not bothered – I can cope. Tough as nails, me.

What's your style like?

Nothing fancy. Jeans, T-shirt and trainers.

You need a cheap, **simple car** that does everything a car needs to do, like the Dacia Sandero or Skoda Roomster.

Designer gear from head to toe.

Ooh yuk! I can't stand getting cold and wet.

How do you get across a playing field?

You need a **convertible** so you can feel the sun on your face. Try a Mazda MX-5.

Running in a zigzag, carrying a bag of golf sticks.

Are you nuts? Just around town is fine.

Running in a straight line, yelling at the top of my voice.

You need a **sporty saloon car** like the BMW M3, as driven by salesmen with Bluetooth earpieces.

Do you often feel the need to go to the other side of the country?

Which of these phrases do you use more often?

You need a huge noisy ridiculous **muscle car**, like a Dodge Camaro.

POWERRRRRRRRRR!

Definitely. Can't stand them.

You don't want a car at all. You want to make something in a shed, like a **caravan airship** or a train.

Actually, I do, for some reason. And then I have to come straight back again.

Hello trees, hello flowers, hello sky... I love you!

The perfect car for you is a huge noisy ridiculous **supercar**, like a V12 Lamborghini.

You want a **grand tourer** – something to get you a very long way in great comfort. Have a look at a Jaguar XJ.

You seem to have chosen an **eco car** – probably something that needs plugging in every night, like the Nissan Leaf.

Donuts or Doughnuts?

They might share a similar sounding name, but which is more fun: making smoky circles in a car, or a batch of delicious, sugary, jammy treats? We put them head-to-head to find out...

Donuts (the car ones)

You'll need a rear-wheel drive car with plenty of power. The very cheapest you'll find is something like a Toyota GT86, which costs nearly £25,000. And then, unless you own a racetrack or a giant car park, you'll need to build yourself a HUGE expanse of tarmac to practise on. Oh, and you'll need a big stack of replacement tyres. And probably a replacement clutch. And an awful lot of petrol. This is going to cost you a lot of cash.

EXPENSE

Doughnuts (the food ones)

Let's see... a bag of flour? A bit of milk, an egg, some flour and a few spoonfuls of sugar? Surely you can find all those in your kitchen cupboard? Even if you have to go out and buy the lot, the ingredients for a giant batch of doughnuts won't cost you more than a few pounds. Definitely better value for money.

Quite high. Even if you've found a giant, deserted stretch of tarmac and there's not another soul within fifty miles, there's still plenty that can go wrong. Your tyres might blow out, or catch on fire... or, worst of all, you might develop Clarkson's Cricked Neck Syndrome from all the G-force of spinning.

DANGER

Cooking doughnuts is more dangerous than you might think. After you've made the dough and rolled it into balls, you need to drop the balls into a pan of very hot oil. Hot oil is dangerous, nasty stuff, which means it's best to get an adult to do this bit. Even so, no one has ever crashed into a ditch while making doughnuts.

Donuts (the car ones)

Doughnuts (the food ones)

Unbelievably, donuts are completely calorie-free! Even if you're on the strictest diet, you can enjoy as many donuts as you want, as many times a day as you can manage! What could be healthier?

CALORIES

Doughnuts are notoriously unhealthy, especially if they're filled with jam and rolled in sugar. Of course, if you just have one or two, that's fine, but who can limit themselves to one or two doughnuts?

A perfect donut is one of the toughest skills to master. Once you've turned the wheel and booted the throttle, you then have to balance the car perfectly between steering and accelerator to keep in a tight spin without sliding out of control. It takes even the finest drivers a lot of practice to get it just right!

DIFFICULTY

Doughnuts are tricky to cook. Don't leave the dough to rise for long enough and they'll be dense and chewy. Don't fry them for long enough and they'll be raw on the inside, fry them for too long and they'll be burned. But after a few batches you'll have them perfect.

Making daft, smoky donuts isn't big and it isn't clever. However, it is very cool. At least, it is until you accidentally put the car into reverse and blow up the engine!

COOLNESS

If you make batch after batch of perfect, jam-filled, sticky-finger doughnuts, your friends will probably be quite impressed. And, eventually, very full of doughnuts. But you'll always be known as 'the one obsessed with baking' rather than 'the one with awesome car control'.

The record for the most consecutive donuts is held by Jamie Morrow of the UK, who performed an amazing 280 spins in his Westfield Sport 1600. Bet he was dizzy by the end of that!

WORLD RECORDS

Lup Fun Yau holds the world record for eating the most sugared jam doughnuts. In 2007 he consumed six doughnuts in three minutes. Doesn't sound like very many, but you try and beat it!

IN CONCLUSION...

Doing donuts – the noisy car-ones – is more expensive, more dangerous, more difficult and much, much cooler than making jammy, sugary doughnuts. And it's healthier for you, too!

HE SAID WHAT?

SOMETIMES IT'S HARD TO WORK OUT QUITE WHAT JEREMY, JAMES AND RICHARD ARE TRYING TO SAY. ESPECIALLY WHEN WE HIDE SOME OF THE WORDS. CAN YOU FILL IN THE BLANKS?

1. SUDDENLY I KNEW WHAT IT FELT LIKE TO BE A ………………… CAUGHT IN THE HEADLIGHTS.

2. I DAREN'T LOOK IN THE MIRROR. IT'S LIKE BEING ATTACKED BY ………………… .

3. JAMES MAY IS – THERE'S NO OTHER WORD FOR IT – ………………… !

4. I DON'T KNOW THAT I WANT TO BE IN A BIG, LOUD V12 ………………… THAT DOESN'T, EVERY NOW AND AGAIN, TRY AND KILL ME. I MISS THAT.

RACE TO THE SOURCE

CAN YOU SPEED ACROSS AFRICA AND FIND THE ORIGIN OF THE WORLD'S MIGHTIEST RIVER BEFORE YOUR OPPONENTS?

You Will Need:

- A playing piece for each player
- A die
- A hammer (optional)

How to Play

Take turns rolling the die and moving the indicated number of spaces around the board, following the instructions (or cheating wildly) as you go. The winner is the first to reach the source of the Nile.

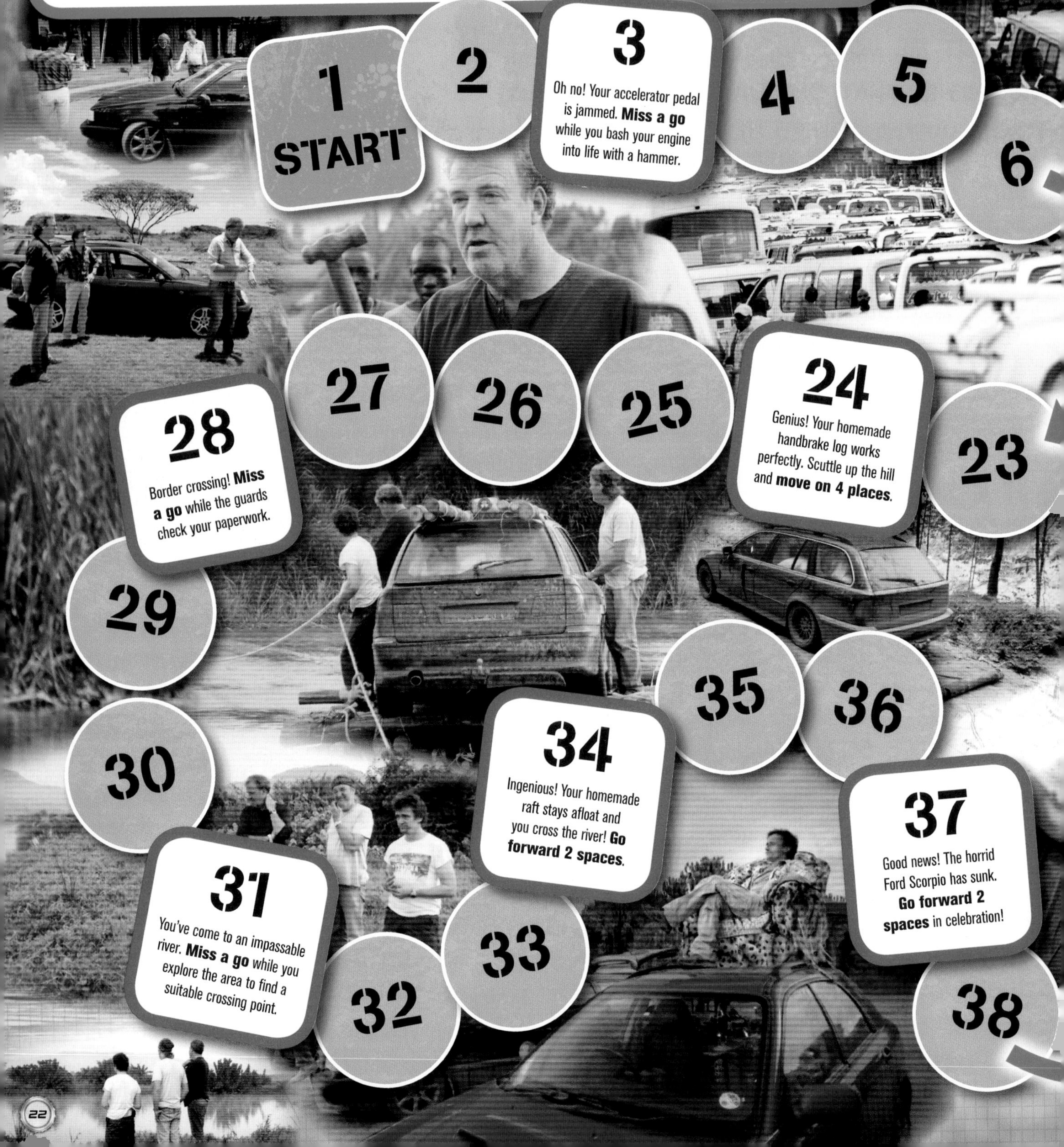

1 START
2
3 Oh no! Your accelerator pedal is jammed. Miss a go while you bash your engine into life with a hammer.
4
5
6
23
24 Genius! Your homemade handbrake log works perfectly. Scuttle up the hill and move on 4 places.
25
26
27
28 Border crossing! Miss a go while the guards check your paperwork.
29
30
31 You've come to an impassable river. Miss a go while you explore the area to find a suitable crossing point.
32
33
34 Ingenious! Your homemade raft stays afloat and you cross the river! Go forward 2 spaces.
35
36
37 Good news! The horrid Ford Scorpio has sunk. Go forward 2 spaces in celebration!
38

OF THE NILE

13
Yuck! Your mates have set a trap and sprayed you with mud! **Miss a go** while you wipe your windscreen.

12

11

10
Yuck! You've checked into the world's dirtiest, most horrible hotel! **Go back 4 spaces** as you suffer the worst night's sleep in history.

9

14

8
A perfectly smooth road! **Zoom forward 4 places** along the lovely bump-free tarmac.

7

15
King of the forest! You cleverly chose the only four-wheel drive car. **Speed forward 3 places** while your rivals wallow in the mud.

19
Crack! A branch falls through your windscreen and smashes it. **Go back 3 places** while you clear out the broken glass.

18

16

17

20

22
Oh dear! Your idiot colleague has hacked a wonky square of metal out of your bonnet to fix his car. **Miss a go** while you neaten up his scruffy handiwork.

21

45

46

47
Bang! Your airbag goes off in a deafening blast. **Miss a go** while your ears stop ringing.

44
Bliss! You fit a fan to the dashboard. **Blast on 2 spaces** in icy comfort.

43

42

48

41
Another flat tyre! **Go back 3 spaces**.

49

40
Flat tyre! **Go back 4 spaces**.

39

50 FINISH
Congratulations! You've found the source of the Nile! Treat your opponents to a sporting handshake... but don't forget to remind them it's YOU who'll go down in history!

DEAR UNCLE CLARKSON...

Top Gear's resident agony uncle solves your life problems with grown-up, sensible advice...

AND A BIG HAMMER.

Dear Uncle Clarkson

I promise I've been paying attention in maths lessons, but no matter how hard I try, I really can't do long division. I just keep getting the answer wrong! Can you help me?

Callum, Preston

Dear Callum,

I sympathise with you. Long division is tricky. The first thing to remember is to write your sum out properly. Put the number you want to divide on the right-hand size, with the number you're wanting to divide it by – usually the smaller one – on the left. Clear so far? Good. Then hit the equation hard with a hammer until it is divided into many smaller pieces. This should stop it from bothering you any more.

Dear Uncle Clarkson

My dad's Skoda Octavia is making a horrible whining noise every time he drives it. I've had a look in the manual and I think it must be either the fan belt or the power steering pump. What should we do about it?

Jimmy, Watford

Dear Jimmy,

Modern cars aren't as easy to fix as they were in the old days. Once upon a time, engines only had a few moving parts, but nowadays they contain dozens of processors, microchips and sensors that can't simply be tweaked with a few spanners. So to fix the problem with your dad's car, you need to do the following. One, read its manual cover-to-cover. Two, get a qualification in car mechanics. Three, hit the engine all over with a large hammer. If you hit it hard enough and for long enough, the whining will eventually stop. So will the engine.

Dear Uncle Clarkson

I'm worried about the global financial situation. As far as I understand it, governments have borrowed far too much money and don't collect enough taxes to repay their debts. Is there any way for Britain to solve this problem?

Jessica, Penzance

Dear Jessica,

There are many different opinions on how to tackle the world's financial downturn. Some economists think government spending must be cut, while others believe we should build lots of new libraries to 'kickstart' the economy. Both are wrong. There's only one solution that will permanently fix this global problem. Collect the debts of every nation... and then hit them really hard with a hammer. Debts eradicated, problem solved!

Dear Uncle Clarkson,
I run a Formula One team, but no matter how much I shout at my drivers, they're always trailing at the back of the grid. I think the problem might be the cars, which I bought cheap from a bloke at the local garage. Is there any way to make them go faster?
Yours,
Sergio, Milan

Dear Sergio,

Formula One is a very complex business. Even the most powerful computers struggle to simulate aerodynamic effects at 200mph speeds, while tiny changes to one part of a car can have unforeseen effects on another. For these reasons, making your F1 car go faster requires an especially large hammer. For safety reasons, please ensure the driver is removed from the car before hammering.

DEAR UNCLE CLARKSON,

I'M BUILDING A WOODEN BIRD TABLE IN OUR GARAGE AT HOME, BUT ONE OF THE NAILS IS STICKING OUT A BIT TOO FAR AND I KEEP SNAGGING MY SHIRT ON IT. IS THERE ANY WAY TO FIX THIS, PERHAPS WITH A COMMON TOOL?

BARRY, NORWICH

**DEAR BARRY,
NO IDEA, SORRY.**

NASCAR vs

Hammond recently discovered there's more to America's favourite motorsport than wearing cowboy hats and turning left. But how does NASCAR stack up against Europe's favourite motorsport, Formula One? Time for a head to head...

	NASCAR	Formula One
Power	**Around 850bhp**	Around 800bhp
Top Speed	210mph	**220mph**
Weight	1500kg	**640kg** *Lighter is always better!*
Year of first championship	**1949**	1950
Tracks	Huge ovals where the drivers only have to turn left	**Complicated tracks with chicanes, hairpins and even right-hand turns**

	NASCAR	Formula One
Number of cars	**Up to 43** *More cars means more overtaking!*	Around 22

Formula One

	NASCAR	Formula One
Most successful driver	**Richard Petty and Dale Earnhardt** *seven championships each*	**Michael Schumacher** *seven championships*

	NASCAR	Formula One
Longest track	Talladega Superspeedway *2.66 miles*	**Spa Francorchamps Belgium,** *4.35 miles*
Longest Race	**603 miles,** *Coca-Cola 600*	190 miles
Clever technology	Erm…	**Kinetic Energy Recovery – a clever system that harvests electrical energy under braking, and Drag Reduction System, a flap on the rear wing that clicks shut when a car gets close to overtaking another**

Final score:
Formula One **6 - 5** NASCAR

A close contest, but the festival of futuristic technology that is F1 wins out in the end. And don't you dare say we picked the categories just so we could award victory to the sport at which Britain excels...

SUPERCAR WORD SEARCH

```
A R E T S D A O R E U Q N I C A D N O Z I N A G A P
S X T F E R R A R I F 1 2 B E R L I N E T T A O U 9
T G T E L U A D N A L H C A B Y A M 1 1 0 P V T D L
O H E 7 7 1 G R E H Y J K I M N O K X F R A C 1 1 N
N Y V F 1 2 F R H V A J U K R F 6 O Z N T G 4 5 R O
M K R E N I G S E G G A G E R A R E Y T W A V G 8 T
A H O R G T H F S D I 1 S 5 7 E N N B 1 D N C F V N
R Y C R 6 7 5 G G T 1 D C N A B A I Q F 4 I Y H 8 E
T J 7 A F V 9 O S 9 S 4 Q E G F V G E N B Z X 8 S R
I B C R V 5 5 0 E D W 1 T F R G 9 S 4 E G O B N P E
N F 4 I C C V H Y D W A A A V T 3 E 7 R S N B 7 Y R
O S 1 E J N C B N Q M L 9 F V N 5 G C A X D A Z D I
N R O N E S C 8 4 I B E E H L V 2 G 2 L 2 A 3 H E N
E W 2 Z R B D J T N 3 4 E I L S G C O C M C N O R I
7 F O O P Q R L Q W F T G 6 7 V U C H M 7 1 7 B S H
7 D P K I J U 2 5 6 G H 7 Y Q X 8 X F O O 2 V B T G
A 5 6 8 D C C B 6 5 4 I H J K L Q R E C N F O P R R
T G S L S Z N E B S E D E C R E M A S L 5 T 2 G O O
Y 4 H S A R H Y 5 6 S N Y U S A R T 3 7 J O 1 2 N B
S T R O P S R E P U S N O R Y E V I T T A G U B I M
7 F 1 7 R O D A T N E V A I N I H G R O B M A L C A
Q H E N N E S S E Y V E N O M G T S P Y D E R P R L
```

2014 C7 CORVETTE
AUDI R8 V8 SPYDER S-TRONIC
ASTON MARTIN ONE -77
BUGATTI VEYRON SUPER SPORTS
FERARRI ENZO
FERRARI F12 BERLINETTA

HENNESSEY VENOM GT SPYDER
KOENIGSEGG AGERAR
KOENIGSEGG CCXR
LAMBORGHINI AVENTADOR
LAMBORGHINI REVENTON
LEXUS LFA
MAYBACH LANDAULET
MCLAREN F1
MERCEDES BENZ SLS GT
PAGANI ZONDA C12F

PAGANI ZONDA CINQUE ROADSTER
PORSCHE 911
SSC ULTIMATE AERO
ZEN VOST1

P45

END PARKING MISERY WITH THE COMPLETELY EXCELLENT P45!

A SPECIAL CAR FOR SPECIAL PEOPLE

New cars get bigger and bigger every year, but roads don't. So finding a parking space is getting harder all the time. But you never need to park the P45 – you just stay in it all the time!

➡ **Go to the theatre** – *enjoy the best seat in the house.*
➡ **Go to the shops** – *your arms are free to reach things on the shelves.*
➡ **Go to the library** – *browse books while gently humming.*
➡ **Go to a restaurant** – *as long as there's outside seating and quite high tables*

The P45 is fully road legal, completely safe and allowed to drive almost everywhere – even motorways*. It's absolutely perfect for every driving situation:

- *Smooth, gentle and practically silent indoors, thanks to two smallish batteries and some electric motors***
- *Swift, responsive and exciting around town, thanks to a noisy little engine and fat blobby tyres****
- *Relaxing and soothing on long journeys*****

NEW!

UNIQUE!

TINY!

LG62 LYF

EVERYONE SHOULD BUY THE P45. IF THERE WAS MORE THAN ONE OF THEM, THEN EVERYONE COULD BUY THE P45. BUT FOR SOME UNKNOWN REASON NOBODY WANTS TO INVEST IN IT, SO THERE'S ONLY THIS ONE... MAKE ME AN OFFER?

PLEASE?

TV's Jeremy Clarkson says:

THE P45 IS COMPLETELY EXCELLENT!

* *Do not, under any circumstances, ever drive the P45 on a motorway unless you want to be terrified. And dead.*
** *Range is severely limited. Changing over to electric power is complicated and takes two hours.*
*** *The P45 has a bit of a stability problem that can probably be sorted out, but until then be prepared for sudden loud noises, jerky wobbling, and banging your face on the windscreen.*
**** *As soon as the train companies convert some of their carriages full of seats to allow space for the P45. Until then, you might find a helpful coach.*

The next day, the boys have a new challenge...

IT SAYS WE WILL HAVE A TEN-LAP RACE OF THE TRACK.

DESERT DEMOLITION DERBY

CHALLENGE

THIS WILL DRIVE ME ROUND THE BEND!

It's the final lap...

OUTTA MY WAY, LOSERS!

EAT MY DESERT DUST!

WATCH OUT— WE'RE GOING TO BE OVERTAKEN!

IT'S THE STIG'S AFRICAN COUSIN!

SOME SAY ... HE'S MADE US LOOK LIKE IDIOTS.

The boys have wrecked their cars.

HOW WILL WE GET TO SOUTH AFRICA NOW?

DON'T PANIC! IN AFRICA, THERE'S ONLY EVER ONE CAR I NEED...

IT'S OLIVER! I LOVE THIS CAR! GET IN, CHAPS!

THIS THING IS OLDER THAN MAY'S HAIRSTYLE!

OLI V3R

Soon the boys are in trouble again ...

HURRY UP! WE'RE BEING CHASED!

HE'S NOT LION, HAMSTER!

AH HA CHAPS, I'VE MADE ONE MEGA MODIFICATION TO OLIVER ...

OLI V3R

TURBO BOOST

How to make your own
Caravan Piñata

YOU WILL NEED

❋ masking tape
❋ double-sided tape
❋ cling film
❋ black, white and silver card
❋ black and white paint
❋ silver pen
❋ string
❋ newspaper
❋ glue
❋ small cardboard box
❋ sweets
❋ scissors

1. Copying the black outline of a caravan template on this page, cut out two caravan sides on white card.

2. Cut a piece of card 115cm long and 22cm wide. Now score a fold line on both long sides 1.5cm from the edge, then cut along both edges to make tabs as shown.

3. Starting at the front, wrap your piece of card around one of the sides of the caravan, folding the tabs over and securing in place with masking tape. Keep going until you reach the front again.

4. Ask an adult to help you cut this shape in half so that your caravan now has a top piece and a bottom piece.

5. Using these pieces as a guide, cut the other caravan side in half to match.

6. Now wrap and fold the tabs onto the other top piece of the caravan side to complete the top of your caravan.

Caravan template

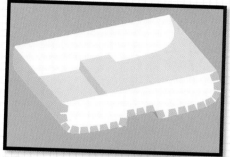

7. Now repeat this process for the bottom half of the caravan.

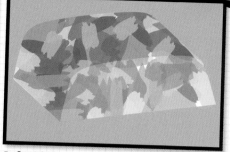

8. Cover both top and bottom caravan pieces with cling film and then cover both pieces with two or three layers of papier mâché and leave to dry.

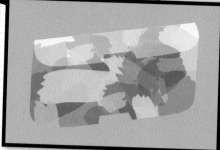

9. Once dry, cover both pieces in another two or three layers of papier mâché and leave to dry.

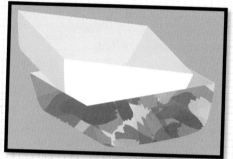

10. When completely dry remove the card mould and cling film from both pieces.

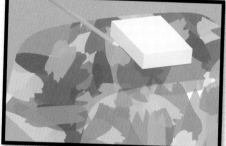

11. To make the skylight opening to pour the sweets into your piñata, take a small cardboard box and place it in the centre of the caravan top, then draw around it.

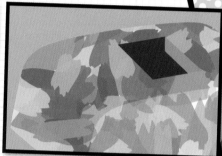

12. Ask an adult to help you cut out the shape you have just drawn, leaving a small tab along one edge.

13. Position the box on the top of the caravan over the hole and using the tab secure in place with tape. This creates a flap that can be lifted in order to fill the caravan with sweets.

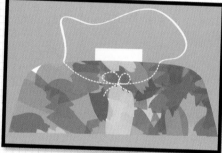

14. Make two small holes in the top of the caravan in order to hang it up. Cut a length of string to thread through the holes, then tie the ends to form a loop.

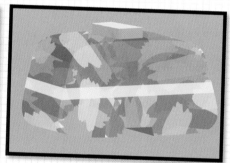

15. Now take the top and bottom halves of your caravan and tape together to form the complete caravan shape.

TOP TIP

Don't make the caravan too sturdy with lots of layers of papier mâché - you're going to need to be able to smash it later!

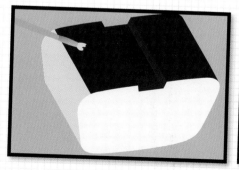

16. Now you can paint your caravan using white paint for the top and black for the bottom of the base as shown.

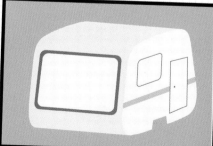

17. Using black and silver paper, stick on shapes for the windows as shown and draw the outline of a door in place.

18. To make the caravan wheels, cut out two circles of about 8cm in diameter. Draw a second circle inside each of these of about 5cm in diameter, then cut around the edge to create tabs as shown. Fold the tabs over.

5cm
8cm

19. Cut a long strip of black card about 2cm wide and apply double-sided tape along one side. Now wrap the strip of card around the circle, sticking it to the tabs as you go. Repeat with the second circle. This will form your wheels.

20. Stick the wheels in place under the wheel arches. Use a silver pen to draw on the detail of the wheels. Your caravan is now ready to be filled with sweets, hung up from the nearest tree and bashed to pieces with a bat, hammer or anything else you fancy.

Spot the Landmark

Last year Jeremy suggested that Audi like to park a Q7 in front of anything interesting that people might want to look at. This turns out to be literally true. Can you name these famous sights that have been mostly spoiled?

HOW DOES THE PAGANI HUAYRA GO SO BLOOMIN' FAST?

In January 2013, Pagani's incredible new hypercar smashed the *Top Gear* lap record, going round in just 1:13.8, over a second quicker than the Ariel Atom V8! But how does it manage such awesome pace? Let's have a look…

FEARLESS DRIVER

There are many fast drivers on this planet, but only one with the superhuman bravery and knowledge of the *Top Gear* test track to extract every last bit of horsepower from the Huayra and shave those vital milliseconds from the lap time! Some say he's the only creature in the world who knows how to pronounce 'Huayra' correctly, and that his liver is made of carbotanium. All we know is, he's called the Stig…

ENGINE

The Huayra uses a custom-built 6.0-litre twin-turbo V12, which makes a stonking 720bhp and 738lb ft – that's more than even the Lamborghini Aventador! It's built for Pagani by the AMG division at Mercedes, the same team that make the V8 in the bruising SLS. So this very Italian hypercar actually has a German heart…

TYRES

Each of the Huayra's specially-made rear tyres measure an astonishing 33 centimetres across – which means over two feet of rubber in contact with the road! Such fat tyres help the Huayra turn all its power into lovely acceleration rather than hopelessly spinning its wheels. Of course, even the biggest tyres will get very smoky if the driver gets too violent with the Huayra's throttle…

FLAPPY THINGS

Most modern hypercars have a big wing or two, but the Huayra goes one better. It has four 'flaps' – two at the front and two at the back – each about the size of this book, which flip up and down to channel air over the car, keeping it flat through the corners. The cleverest bit is that the Huayra does this completely automatically, sensing whether a driver is accelerating or braking, or turning left or right, and popping the right combination of flaps to help the car stick perfectly to the track.

EK·650VV

REAR-WHEEL DRIVE

Just like an F1 car, the Huayra's engine drives its rear wheels only. Compared to a four-wheel drive machine like the Veyron, this saves weight and gives the driver more control over how 'sideways' the car will go. Of course, you need a mighty fine driver to keep that much power under control…

EXOTIC MATERIALS

Other hypercars might be built of carbon fibre or titanium, but only the Huayra is made of CARBOTANIUM! It's a blend of carbon fibre and titanium that's not only incredibly light, but also incredibly strong… oh, and incredibly expensive! Might help to explain why the Huayra costs £660,000…

EK 650VV

GULLWING DOORS

OK, these don't TECHNICALLY help the Huayra to go any faster, but they look cool – surely that counts for a few milliseconds!

A-MAZE-ingly slow!

Help Captain Slow find his way through this maze of roads as quickly as possible.

START

The NEW WORLD'S CAR

Smallest

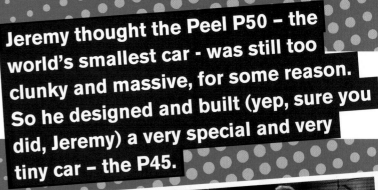

Does this count as a car? Apparently, yes. You don't have to wear a helmet, it has indicators and headlights and a tax disc. So it must be a car. Underneath it's a little quad bike with a two-stroke 100cc engine and a top speed of about 35mph.

GRRRRRRR! GRRRRRRR!

CLUNK! CLUNK!

Jeremy didn't really get in the P45 – he just put it on, like a jacket. Then after a little go on the *TG* track, he took it out on the real road. It performed perfectly, apart from wobbling violently with a loud grinding noise every now and then.

'**Wooaah God!** If you're watching this in the edit, make sure that doesn't go on television. I don't want people thinking this is a **deathtrap**.'

Jeremy had fitted the basic P45 with a couple of options – a manual wash-wipe system for £1.99 (a sponge) and a satnav system for £500 (Jeremy's phone). On the whole, Jeremy was really pleased with his creation.

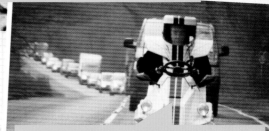

'I can't believe how quiet the roads are this morning. **I'm barely seeing any traffic at all**.'

He could sneak to the front of traffic queues – the P45 really seemed quite good for short journeys in town. How would it cope with a longer trip?

'**The speed machine** is coming through! **Oh yes**. This is **incredible**. Ladies and gentlemen, you're witnessing the **birth of the future**.'

He filled the tank completely (1.7 litres) and took it onto a busy dual carriageway, heading for London. Within seconds he realised this was a bad idea. A very bad idea.

BEEP! BEEP! BEEP! BEEP! BEEP!

He was too terrified to carry on, so he loaded the P45 onto a coach instead and had a soothing hot beverage. When he got to London, he decided to do a bit of shopping. The P45 had one big advantage over the Peel P50 – it could reverse out of lifts.

'Aargh! I've never been **frightened** of a **Citroen Picasso** before and I just was! **Aaargh!** Got a weave on... **Aargh! Help me! Help!** How fast is that now? Thirty-four? **Lorry! Lorry! Lorry! Aargh!**'

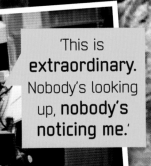

'This is **extraordinary.** Nobody's looking up, **nobody's noticing me.**'

Even better, the P45 is actually a hybrid. Jeremy could convert it to run off batteries in a few minutes. Well – two handy men could convert it, in 116 minutes. The P45 was now very, very quiet, but it would only trundle about for a couple of hours. That was plenty of time for Jeremy to finish his shopping and go to the library.

But Jeremy spent too long in the library, and the batteries went flat. The P45 is much heavier than the Peel P50, so he couldn't carry it out. He had to start the petrol engine.

That evening, Jeremy went to the theatre, in his P45. This worked very well, apart from not having quite enough room to eat popcorn comfortably. The next day, Jeremy was certain the P45 was completely excellent in every way. So he set off for a meeting with some potential financial backers to see if he could make lots more P45s... after a quick wash.

Unfortunately the meeting didn't go well. They gave him his P45 back.

VRMM VRUMM VRUMM

'This is so **embarrassing**. Sorry. **Sorry everybody**. I'm so sorry.'

'Aah, it's **not warm!** It's extremely **cold!** Oh, it's gone quite badly... What's happened here? A **terrible thing** has **happened.**'

It turned out the P45 was a stupid idea. Sorry, Jeremy.

'...It's **got stripes** on it...'

45

Cars of the Future...

Ever wondered how cars will look in twenty years' time? You don't need a crystal ball or a time machine to find out. Check out the cars of today that are decades ahead of their time...

TODAY!

Honda FCX Clarity

It might be a big family car with a Honda badge on the front, but it's what's under the Clarity's sensible bodywork that's truly futuristic. It runs on liquid hydrogen, which reacts in the FCX's fuel cell with oxygen from the air to make lots of lovely electricity. The only thing that comes out the exhaust is clean, unpolluting water – no sooty carbon dioxide or harmful greenhouse gases. So what's the downside? You'll have to drive all the way to California to find a hydrogen refuelling station. And that's a pretty long way if you live in, say, Birmingham...

Porsche 918

In the past, hybrids were boring, sensible cars driven by people who wore cardigans and talked about long division. But in the future, hybrids will be the most exciting cars on the roads. Just look at the amazing Porsche 918 hypercar, which – just like the Prius – gets its power from both a petrol engine and an electric motor. But unlike the Prius, the 918 is seriously fast and insanely expensive: with a 580bhp V8 engine plus two electric motors making a combined 243bhp, it can do 0-60mph in 2.8 seconds and 202mph flat-out...

BMW Gina

When you think about it, metal's not really a very good material to make a car from. It's heavy, it rusts, and it costs lots to repair when an OAP bumps her Nissan Micra into your car at 1mph in the supermarket car park. So why not make cars from fabric? Sounds crazy, but that's exactly what's stretched over the frame of BMW's 'Gina' concept: a skin made of lycra, the stuff used to make leotards! It'll never rust, can change shape depending on the frame beneath it... and best of all, if MicraNan drives into it, you can just iron out the crease. But it is just a concept car, so you can't actually buy it...

BMW i8

The science of aerodynamics isn't only important for Formula One engineers. How cleanly your road car slips through the air makes a huge difference to how fast it'll go, and how much fuel it'll burn. And BMW's new i8 sports car shows the future of aero. Look at all those overlapping panels and wings, which allow the car to swoosh smoothly through the air rather than battering into it like Clarkson's Citroën motorhome! Such clever aero means the i8 doesn't need a huge engine: it's powered by a dinky three-cylinder petrol engine and an electric motor. And, best of all, it looks pretty cool too... But it's not available yet either...

Citroën GT

Real-world cars often make their way into the virtual world of computer games. But in the future, this journey might just turn back-to-front. When the Citroën team created the mad, swoopy GT concept for the Gran Turismo 5 racing game on the Playstation, the car got such a reaction from gamers that they decided to make it for real. Just think: one day you might be able to design your perfect car on your computer, email the plans off to Citroën - and a few weeks later it'll turn up on your driveway! Hopefully it'll be a bit cheaper than the GT, though – Citroën built just six, each of which cost around two million quid...

Volkswagen L1

Even the most efficient diesel-powered cars today can only go eighty miles or so on a gallon of fuel. But what about a car that could do nearly 200 miles to the gallon? Sounds impossible, but that's exactly what VW's experimental L1 does. Taking fourteen seconds to reach 60mph, it's not especially fast, but it does at least have seating for two - and it's narrow enough to squeeze through the nastiest city traffic jam! And if you just used it to potter around town, you'd only need to fill up the L1 about once a year...

Mercedes SLS E-Cell

Don't worry, there'll still be plenty of fast, shiny, expensive supercars in the future. But they might not be powered by big, noisy V8s. Merc's SLS E-Cell doesn't have a single cylinder, or exhaust pipe, or even a fuel tank: it runs on electric power only. The problem with most previous electric cars is that they've been too slow and can't go very far before they run out of juice. But the SLS certainly won't be slow. With 526bhp and a ridiculous 649lb ft of torque it'll do 0-60mph in less than four seconds and 197mph flat-out... and it should manage over 150 miles between recharges. If you drive it carefully. Which you won't.

Google Driverless Car

Bet you always thought Google was only good for telling you how many goldfish there are in China, or how to boil a sausage? Well, Google does a lot more than search engines. For nearly a decade, the Google boffins have been beavering away to create a completely driverless car. That's right: this dull-looking Prius can motor itself around busy city streets, avoiding pedestrians and cars and somehow managing not to crash. How? With a super-futuristic array of sensors, radar, sat nav and computer power. Google's human-free car is just a prototype (though it's road-legal in some American states) but experts think it could be less than a decade until we see the first fully driverless car on sale... But where's the fun in not being able to drive it yourself?

DRAW
TG's Favourite Cars

USE THESE SKETCHES TO PRACTISE DRAWING SOME OF OUR FAVOURITE CARS, THEN HAVE A GO AT CREATING YOUR OWN CONCEPT CARS OF THE FUTURE...

HiLUX

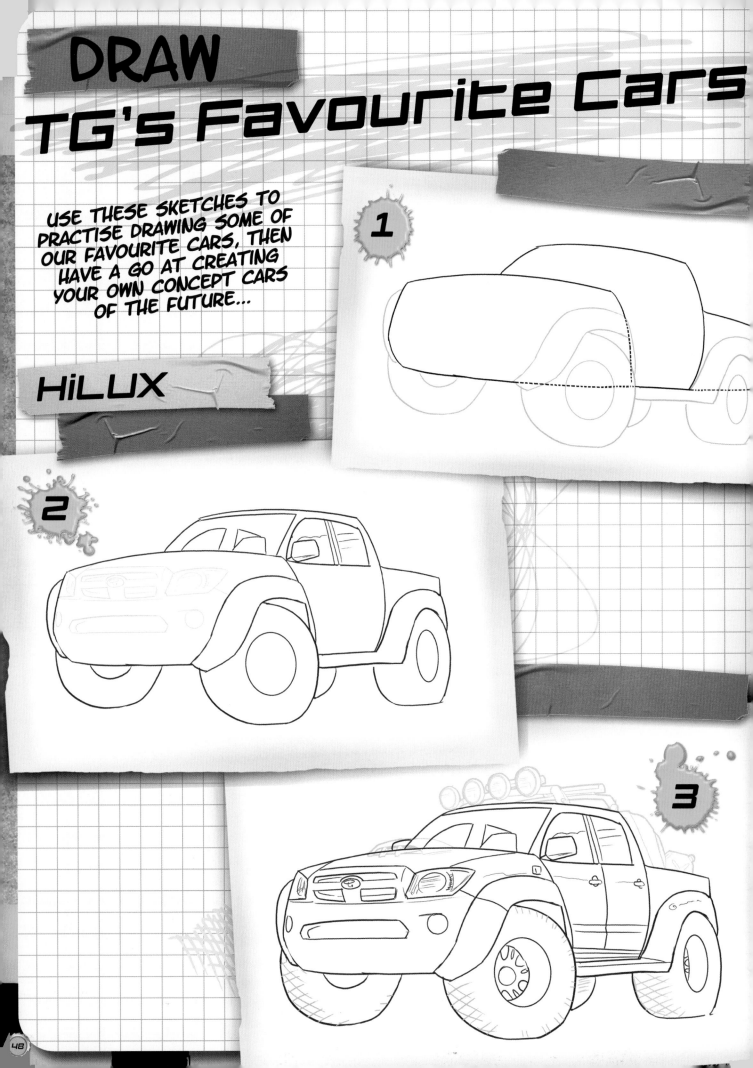

1

2

3

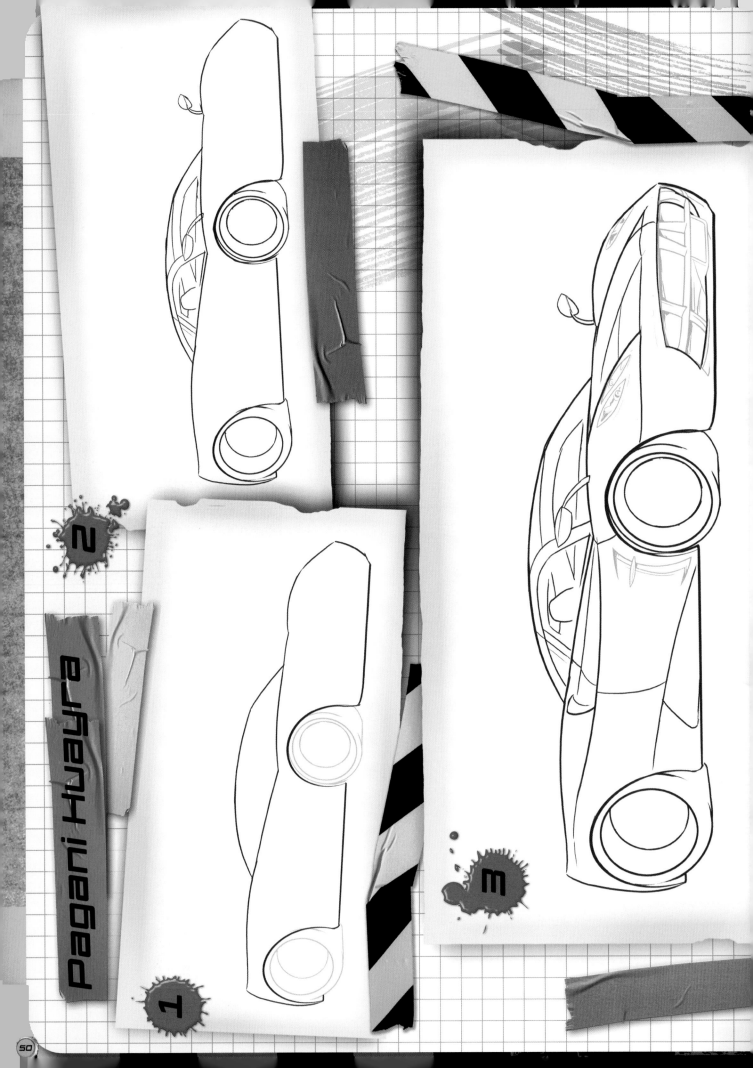

Pagani Huayra

1

2

3

Are Trackday Cars Any Good?

You go to a racetrack, pay a few quid and get to race around for the day. How cool is that? Very, that's how cool. But what is the best kind of trackday car to do it in? And are they any good when you're not on the racetrack? The chaps went to the Donington Track to find out.

James went old-school, unsurprisingly. The Caterham 7 Superlight R500 is a recent version of a car that's been around for over fifty years.

Jeremy went scarily modern and hi-tech.

'This is the **KTM X-Bow***. Part **insect**, part terrain-following **missile**.'

It had push-rod actuated double-wishbone suspension, which he thought was good even though he didn't know what it meant.

'It's **simple**, it's **pure**, it's an unadulterated **driving experience** and I absolutely **love it**.'

*That's pronounced 'crossbow', not 'ex-bow'. We're here to help.

Then Richard turned up in a wooden aeroplane with no wings and only three wheels. The engine wasn't even inside the car. Jeremy wasn't impressed.

The first test was to see who was fastest from 0 to 100mph and back to 0 again. And to make it more fun, they had to do a Le Mans start – they had to run to their cars and climb in before driving off.

'**Running?** It's not a school sports day. Do you have an egg and a spoon? **I hate running**. This is just **stupid**.'

'It's an **action tricycle**.'

Richard in his action tricycle finished before Jeremy even managed to start the complicated X-Bow. So they tried again… and again… and again.

Jeremy thought his X-Bow could corner fastest – and he managed 69.41mph. Then James had a go in the Caterham…

'How **hard** can it be…'

Eventually, James thought he'd won – but he'd only got up to 100kmh, not 100mph. While he tried to impress Jeremy with numbers, Richard did a few laps, desperately trying to get up to anywhere near 100mph.

'What do we call him, what's his **nickname?**'

'Captain... **Captain Quick?**'

'**No**, it isn't that.'

Then they had a go at doughnuts, which Jeremy hoped Richard wouldn't manage. Jeremy couldn't get his huge tyres to slide much, but James did pretty well. And then…

'Ladies and gentlemen, **sit back** and prepare to **laugh your ears off**.'

But he could. He really could.

They gave up on stupid tests, and helped themselves to a big bucket of fun by just driving round the track in the sunshine. Richard was so happy he started to sing.

'As Hammond **does a dough**. He's only got **one wheel**, so he **can't** do a **whole doughnut**.'

'Jeremy's hit the gravel, **ha-ha ha-ha haa-hah**!'

'Just **brilliant**. You and your **mates**, just belting around, indulging your **passion for cars**.'

They had a blast, but unfortunately that's only part of the trackday experience. You have to get to the track on normal roads. So the chaps were told to drive from London to the *TG* track. They felt very exposed and self-conscious in town.

Then it got much, much worse… thanks to a bit of rain and a chilly breeze.

'My right hand is **completely frozen**, it's just a **claw**. Also, there are **holes** in the **floor** behind the pedals, and all the air and the **wind** and the **rain** is **going up my** trouser legs.'

'You feel a **bit of a berk**, to be honest. A lot of people will be driving past and their children will be saying, '**Daddy, why has that man's windscreen** fallen off?"

'**Ow!** Ow, ow! **Mega-ow!** Oh God, I **need a hat** or something!'

In the end, they had to dress up like cuddly astronauts to manage the last twelve miles. They got to the *TG* production office in a bit of a state.

'The **bit of your face** that's exposed has **gone all funny**. It's got mud and bits of stones on it.'

Trackday Cars: The Verdict

POSITIVES

↘ **Enormous fun**
↘ **Relatively cheap and simple**
↘ **Anyone can have a go**

NEGATIVES

↘ **No roof, windscreen, heater, doors, windows, storage space…**
↘ **Bit tricky over speed bumps (Morgan)**
↘ **Ridiculously complicated to start and a terrible turning circle (X-Bow)**
↘ **Absolutely useless in bad weather (all of them)**

Rocket Power!

BALLOON ROCKET

A rocket is sent flying by the exhaust gas which is pushed out by the burning fuel. Have a go a making a balloon fly by using the same principle.

1. Thread a length of string through a straw.

2. Now attach one end to the top of your banister so that the string hangs down from the top floor. The end of the string should be long enough to reach the ground floor.

3. Blow up a balloon and, whilst holding the neck closed, tape the balloon to the straw. Ensure that the opening of the balloon is facing towards the ground.

4. Once the balloon is attached to the straw, let go of the end so the air is released. Watch as your rocket rushes upwards!

YOU WILL NEED:
• Ball of string
• Balloon
• Tape

N.B. If you don't have any stairs you can do the same experiment by tying the string between two chairs.

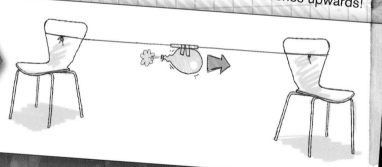

THE EXPLODING DRINK BOTTLE

YOU WILL NEED:
• A large bottle of diet cola
• Half a packet of Mentos

1. Stand the cola bottle in the middle of an open outdoor space and slowly undo the lid.

2. Quickly drop one or two Mentos down into the bottle.

3. Take cover!

A TOWERING ERUPTION OF DIET COLA SHOULD BURST OUT OF THE BOTTLE!

Scientists are still trying to thrash this out, but the cola eruption is believed to be caused by the carbon dioxide and chemicals in the drink combined with the little bumps on the surface of the Mentos. This will only work with diet drinks as they contain the right combination of chemicals.

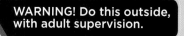

WARNING! Do this outside, with adult supervision.

Accessories

A chap needs accessories for driving in style. Take your pick between the Stig mask for days when you want to go faster, or the goggles and compass for a more gentle drive in the country...

The Stig Mask

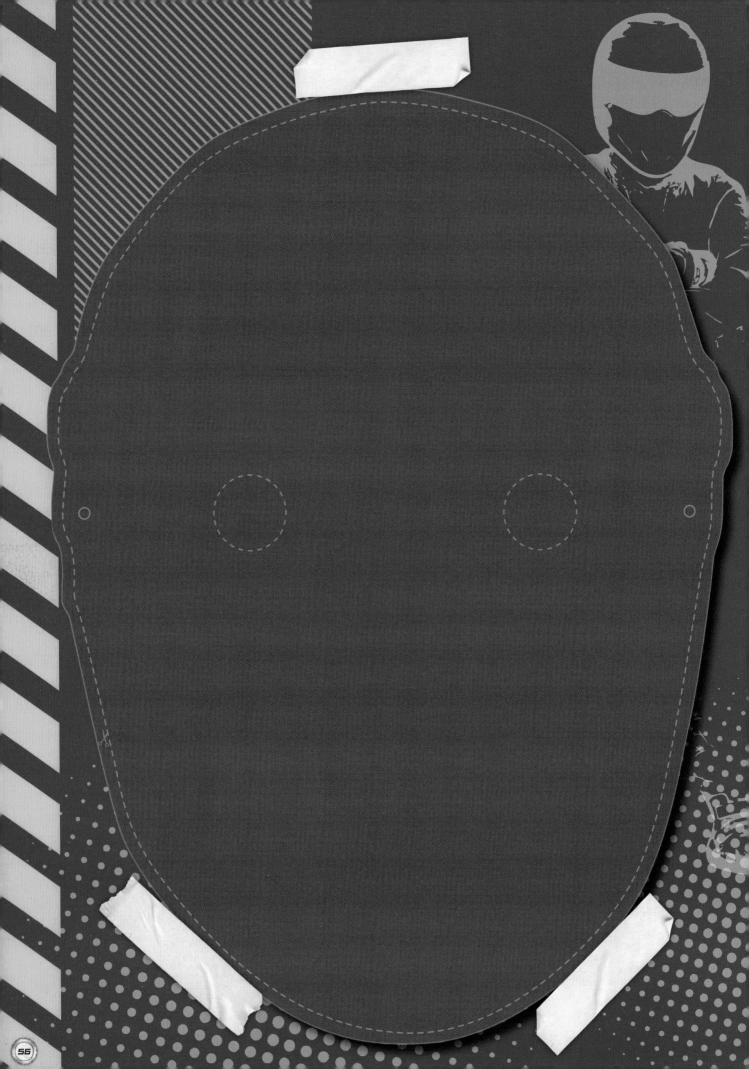

Goggles For Chaps

Don't forget to cut out the eye holes in the Stig mask and the goggles, otherwise you may find they don't work quite as well as they should...

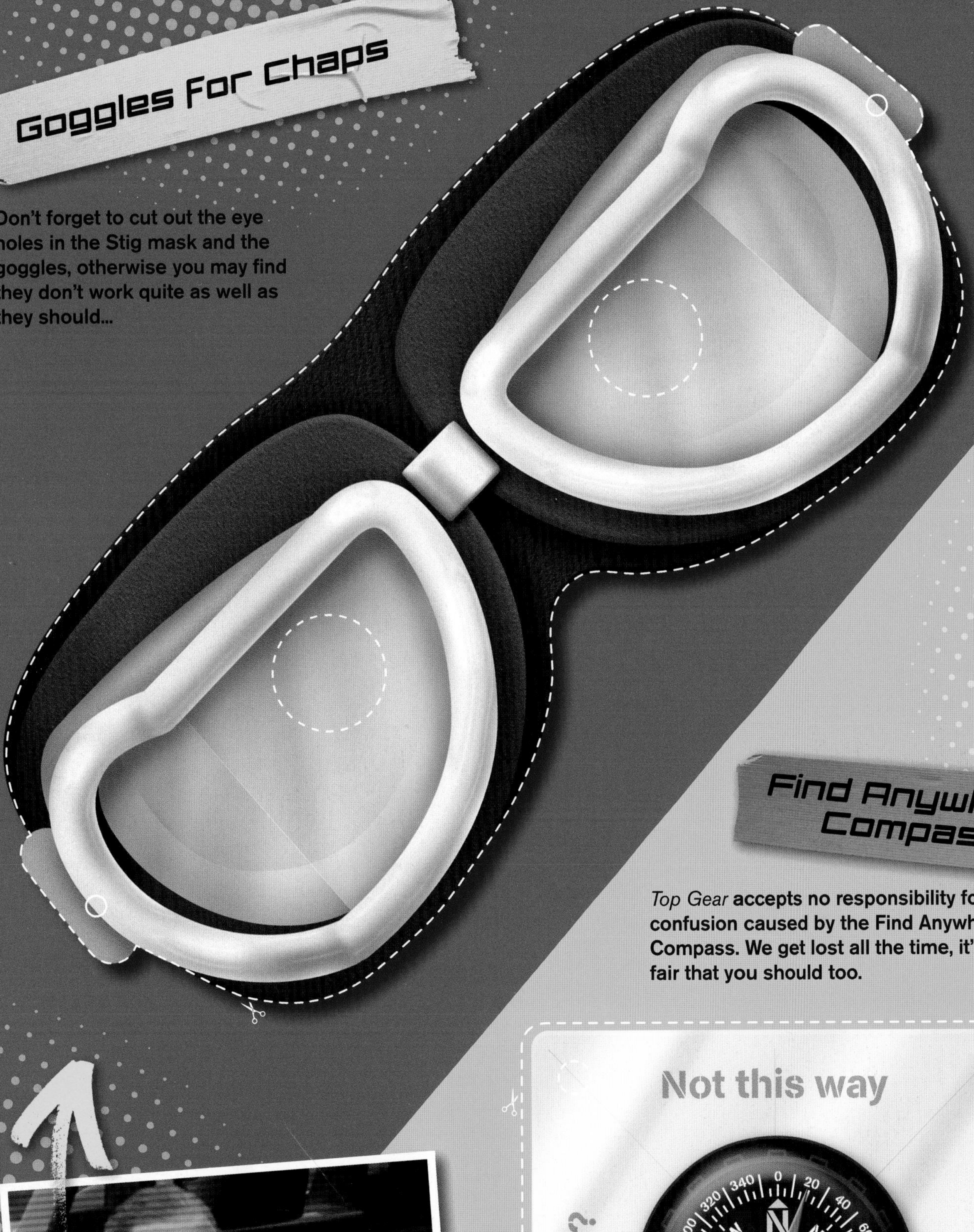

Find Anywhere Compass

Top Gear accepts no responsibility for any confusion caused by the Find Anywhere Compass. We get lost all the time, it's only fair that you should too.

Not this way

Where?

Eek!

Surely not

Spot the Difference

Find twenty differences between these two pictures.

Bling my Bentley

James got a bit confused giving directions to rally driver Kris Meeke in a Bentley Continental GT Speed. But they made it through the rally stage without crashing... and they weren't last. (They were second-to-last.)

THIS IS THE FIVE, YOU'RE TOO LATE, JAMES! *COME ON!*

RIGHT, SQUARE RIGHT. SORRY, SQUARE LEFT.

WOAH! JAMES, EITHER GET IT RIGHT OR *SHUT UP!*

FIVE RIGHT INTO SIX LEFT AND THEN FORTY METRES. INTO FIVE RIGHT.

JAMES, I'M GOING TO GO OFF THE ROAD IF YOU DON'T CALL THE NOTES!

After the stage, the car needed a good wash. Can you help by working out which of these mudsplats are not on this Bentley Continental?

1 2 3 4 5 6 7 8 9 10

Answers

Page 20
He Said What?
1. Rabbit
2. Tigers
3. Winning
4. Lambo
5. Sleeping bag
6. Noble
7. Orange dog
8. Nurburgring
9. Pagani Zonda
10. Bear

Page 39
Spot the Landmark
1. The Angel of the North
2. Eiffel Tower
3. Pyramids
4. Statue of Liberty
5. Leaning Tower of Pisa
6. Big Ben
7. Sydney Opera House
8. Stonehenge
9. Taj Mahal
10. Mount Rushmore

Page 60
Bling my Bentley
Splats 2 and 9 are not on the car

Page 28
Supercar Word Search

Page 59
Spot the Difference

Page 42
A-MAZE-ingly Slow

VRRRAAAAAAH
VRRRAAAAAAH

KAS
189

OLI V3R

STOP

TG

DIRECT HOME DELIVERY
DHD
DAF
XF